Red Star and Blue Star Defeat Spexman

Randy Lewis - K'ayaxan
and
William Layman

Native River Fund
Wenatchee Valley Museum & Cultural Center
Wenatchee, Washington

DEDICATION

Rodney Daut

Mary A. Miller Marchand who shared
her deep spiritual relationship with the land,
her people and the Creator.

Wenatchee Valley
Museum

& Cultural Center

Copyright ©2018 by the Native River Fund of the Wenatchee Valley Museum
& Cultural Center. All rights reserved. No part of this book may be used or
reproduced in any manner whatsoever without written permission except in
the case of brief quotations embodied in reviews. For information contact:
Wenatchee Valley Museum & Cultural Center, 127 S. Mission, Wenatchee,
WA 98801. Website address: www.wenatcheevalleymuseum.org.

ISBN 978-0-578-41128-6

Printing supported by Community Foundation of NCW.

Cover Photograph: Edward Layman
Back Cover Photograph: William Layman

Printed by Commercial Printing, Inc.
Wenatchee, Washington

GRATITUDES

This book evolved from a cultural landmarks tour given by Randy Lewis (K'ayaxan) for the Wenatchee Valley Museum & Cultural Center's 2012 museum exhibit, River of Baskets: Columbia River Tribal Basketmakers.

A special appreciation goes to the museum's Native River Fund which provided financial support to K'ayaxan so his voice and words could come alive on these pages.

We are grateful to Susan Evans for her encouragement and help in keeping the project moving along. Also we thank Jake Lodato for his excellent editing, Scott Reynolds for his printing expertise, and the Community Foundation of NCW for the publication's printing.

A very big thanks goes to the Colville Tribal Language Program, and specifically, to Sharon Covington and Ernie Brooks who translated Salish words from the Wenatchi/P'Squosa dialect for placement into the story.

Lastly, we wish to honor the living legacy of Jerome Miller and all Wenatchi/P'Squosa people who keep their culture strong.

Randy Lewis
William Layman
Wenatchee, Washington

William Layman

The Salmon People
Peshastin Pinnacles State Park

INTRODUCTION

WILLIAM LAYMAN

CULTURAL LANDMARKS
OF THE P'SQUOSA / WENATCHI

The lands surrounding the confluence of the Wenatchee and Columbia Rivers are made of sandstone, granite and basalt – broken and worn by glaciation, rivers and time.

Certain outcrops are Beings, placed here before humans in the time of the Animal People.

THE OWL SISTERS

Along the road to Malaga, two pillars stand against the skyline. They are known from time immemorial as the Owl Sisters. The dreaded sisters grabbed young ones and stuck them into their baskets so they could be roasted.

To Wenatchi/P'squosa Indians such landmarks were placed on the land by the Creator. Their teachings form a foundation of regional identity that remains strong.

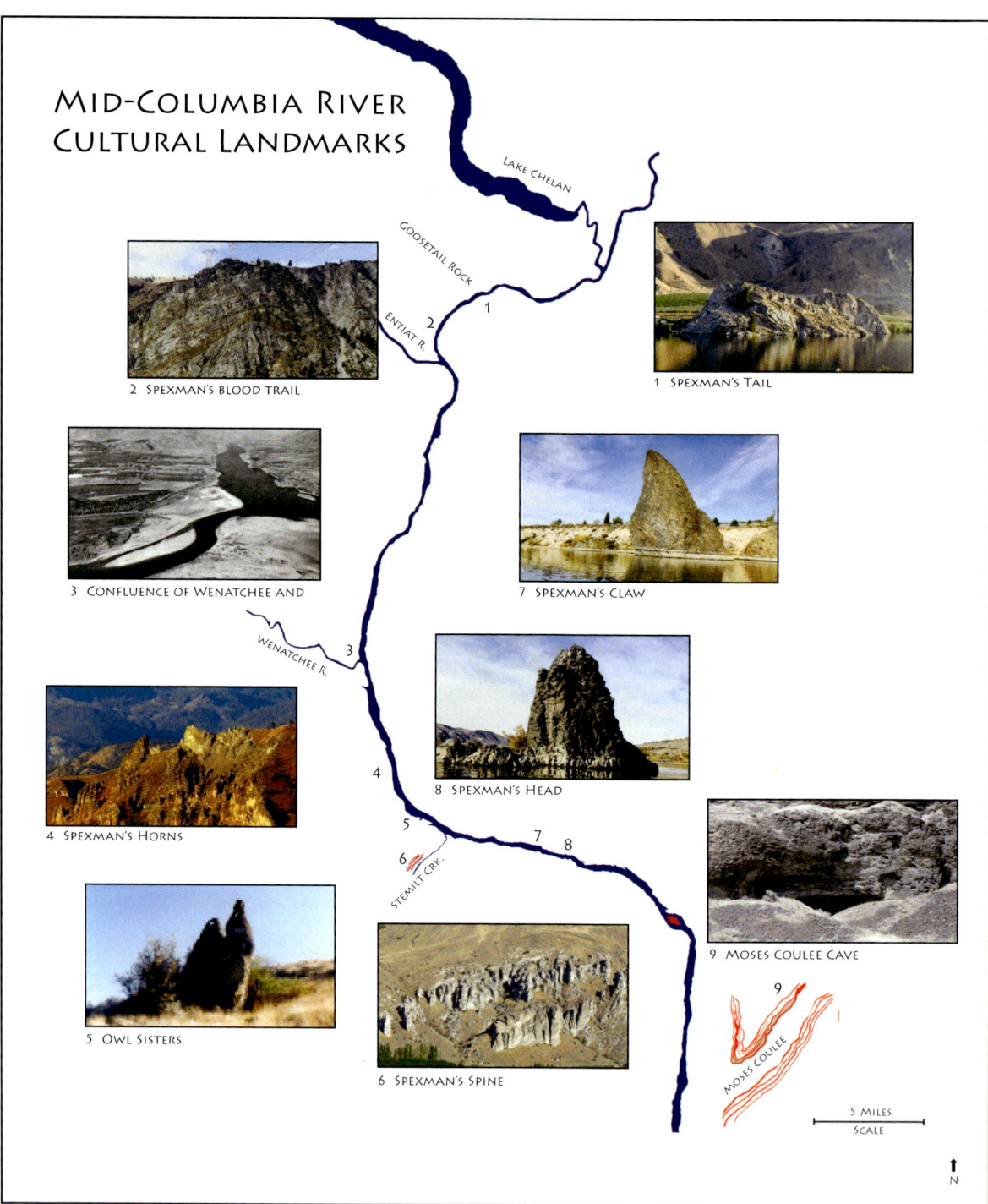

MID-COLUMBIA RIVER CULTURAL LANDMARKS

LAKE CHELAN

GOOSETAIL ROCK

ENTIAT R.

WENATCHEE R.

STEMILT CRK.

2 SPEXMAN'S BLOOD TRAIL

1 SPEXMAN'S TAIL

3 CONFLUENCE OF WENATCHEE AND

7 SPEXMAN'S CLAW

4 SPEXMAN'S HORNS

8 SPEXMAN'S HEAD

9 MOSES COULEE CAVE

5 OWL SISTERS

6 SPEXMAN'S SPINE

MOSES COULEE

5 MILES
SCALE

N

CHIEF EAGLE

Wenatchee Valley residents appreciate the rich textures of our region's geology and landscapes. We are blessed with long views across the treeless canyons and can watch the ever-changing play of light and shadow on the hills. Above Rocky Reach, Abraham Lincoln's face can be seen above the river. Native People see Chief Eagle. Here a boy loved to feed eagles. When his people left him to go to the mountains, the eagles brought the boy food, furs and treasures. After their return, the villagers realized he possessed great power and made him Chief Eagle.

Time stretches back and is written into the landscape. The very DNA of the region's Native Americans joins with Kennewick Man who walked here along the river nine thousand years ago.

As with Chief Eagle, many features and rocks along the Columbia carry specific stories of places. Above Wenatchee, Black Bear and Grizzly Bear can be seen squaring off with one another. Tired of their ceaseless bickering, Coyote turned them into stone.

TWO BEARS FIGHTING

The story told in these pages links revered cultural landmarks up and down the river. It takes place at a critical moment in the time before humans inhabited the land. When Red Star and Blue Star emerge from the cave of their initiation, Coyote charges them with the daunting task of confronting and slaying the water monster Spexman. The boys rise to the occasion, but not before experiencing the full wrath of the monster. Their valor makes the world safe for future beings to come.

Mythological time surrounds us. The rock formations and their stories here offer an essential teaching – that we may be called take on a difficult undertaking for the benefit of others. There are, after all, monsters that still need to be slayed. Red Star and Blue Star affirm it can be done. K'ayaxan gifts us all by remembering and sharing this knowledge.

Noticing these riverplaces brings these landmarks to life. Traveling along the river will never be the same.

SPEXMAN'S HEAD

William Layman

Red Star and Blue Star Defeat Spexman

Randy Lewis ~ K'ayaxan

Below the Wenachee Valley (nṗəsqʷaẁs) there lived a huge and terrifying water monster, Spexman. Spexman lived within the waters of the Columbia River (nṗkʷátkʷ). He had lived through all the previous ages, known to us as houses. We are entering the seventh house, the house made of light, where seeing is believing. From the past eras, there was always a carryover. From the age of the giant mammals came Sasquatch (šc̓wanáẏtəxʷ). He stayed. Creator always left a talisman from the past, to remind us that we were not the first. From the very beginning, at the very beginning was Spexman. Spexman was a dragon. He lay just below the water's surface. Anything that came down the Columbia and Wenatchee Rivers, he grabbed and devoured. He took everything. Herds of animals would disappear when they came downriver. Entire runs of fish were devoured when they came through. Everything that came downriver was his. The Creator was tired of this. He had to move Spexman. The Creator didn't kill his beings. He moved them onto the next plane. He moved them into the next house. Previously Spexman had always managed to duck, dodge and avoid this fate.

CONFLUENCE OF WENATCHEE AND COLUMBIA RIVERS

In a time long ago, the First Ancestors were known as the Animal People (šxitmaškínt). At a major encampment down by the confluence of the Wenatchee and Columbia Rivers, a young woman gave birth to twins (naʔšəšáĺ); this happened in an age when Indians didn't have twins. This happened. Their names were Red Star (čəkʼpəkʼpəkʼyáwt) and Blue Star (qʷiypəkʼpəkʼyáwt).

Everyone – all the Animal People had come – some from great distances to this great meeting place. The Salmon People (ntitiyáx̱ škint) came; they swam upriver to attend. They too had heard of this large gathering. The Salmon People were powerful, very powerful medicine people. Soon after they arrived, they cast a spell on everybody. They put everybody into a trance and in that trance, they stole away the Twins – they stole away Red Star and Blue Star.

MOSES COULEE CAVE

They brought the Twins to this place called Moses Coulee (ncux). In Moses Coulee there was a huge cave. The Salmon People brought them there – hid them in the cave. Deep into this cave they went. Over the years, everyone wondered what happened to the Twins. They thought that maybe the Star People (pə́kpəkyáwt_škint) came down and brought them back, took them back to the heavens.

No, they were growing. They were growing underground, being raised in this place, being reared in total darkness. One by one, animals would show up. They would come into the cave and would spend time with Blue Star and Red Star. They would sing. *ha hey ha hey ya hey ya ha / ha hey ha hey ya hey ya ha / ha hey ha hey ya hey ya ha.* Oh .... that's one of the animals singing. He is singing the song of power that he had. It was Elk (t̓xac̓). In comes another one, *ha hey ha hey ya hey ya ha / ha hey ha hey ya hey ya ha / ha hey ha hey ya hey ya ha.* It was Shrew. Shrew and Mole (púl̓ya) were teaching them about the power of everything that grows underground – telling them of the stone, of the medicine, of the roots, of the poison that these roots held. Field mouse (kʷkʷátna?), not to be left out, shared her vast knowledge of the seeds and grain foods. Cricket (šár̓šar̓') and Grasshopper (c̓aan̓c̓aan̓) sang their jumping songs and medicine songs that teach how to move through daylight and darkness. The Twins were learning, absorbing all these teachings. The Animal People took their turns visiting the cave – one by one the animals gave their Spirit Powers (šúmáx) to Red Star and Blue Star. As they grew, Blue Star and Red Star remembered all the stories, all the songs, all the teachings – everything shared was shared with them. They remembered the smell, the taste of what was underneath and above the ground. In this time, they were being prepared for the day when they would go on top of the land, a place they had not yet seen.

MOSES COULEE

Bruce McCammon

After a great while, the Twins hear this voice – it is the voice of their adopted parents. And they tell them. It's time, it's time to make way for Mankind (skint). At that point, you see, man had no power. Man was an empty brown shell walking around, savaging off the other animals, taking whatever he could.

The Twins are brought forward from the Dark – gradually, they are brought closer to the cave's entrance.

The light gets brighter and brighter as they step closer to the lip of the cave. Finally, Blue Star and Red Star are there. At first, they are blinded, the light is so intense. After a spell, their eyes adjust until they focus on what's before them. The first thing they see is their adoptive parents. They behold the Ant People (kəp̓kip̓múl_škint). Ant People raised them! We give great respect to ants. They are older than the Ancient People, the Old Ones – they came even before we arrived. Right after Spexman came the Ant People. These were giants. They tell Blue Star and Red Star,

>*Your next step lies outside. This is where we have to leave you.*
>*And out they came – the Twins came into the world.*

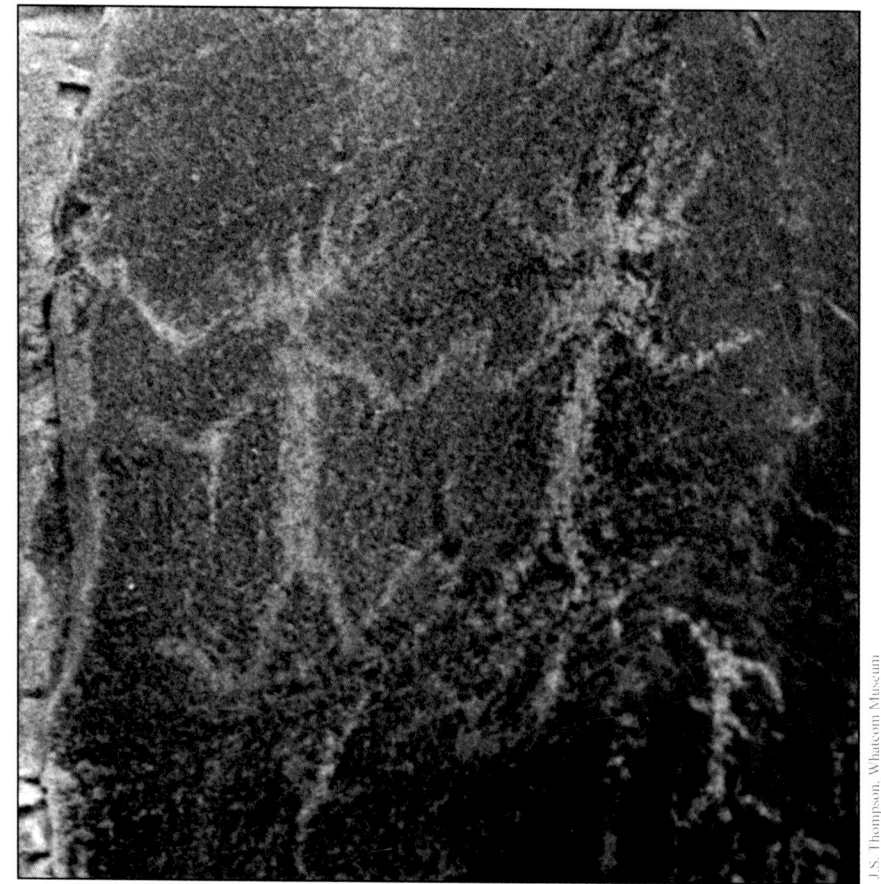

COLUMBIA RIVER PETROGLYPH

And who's there waiting for them? Yup. Ole Coyote (šmiyáw). Oh my, Coyote is so happy. He recognizes them. These are my children that I last saw. And then he tells them, *You know you have a greater purpose on this land (ʔəmʔúmt) right now*. He says, *but first what we have to do is fashion some tools (ḥawiymíntn) for you.*

So, knowing the hardest, sharpest stones, stones that would not break… they fashioned these long points. They made throwing spears we now call atlatl. We didn't have bow and arrows, this was before

bow and arrows. My grandpa used to tell me, "Those points that you call Clovis points, that's when they were made." And he cached them all around in the valley here. Everywhere. In the mountains, they put them, to where they needed them, where People could access them.

Coyote is thinking, he says, *Now, we have to figure out how we're going to get Spexman. He's only vulnerable in one area, and that is underneath where he is softer. There's this little bird you have to get by. His name is Sparrow Hawk (Liklik) and he lives on top of Spexman's head. When Spexman is under water his horns stick up from the river and that is where the little hawk sits.*

Every morning Sparrow Hawk rises into the air and hovers, scanning the horizon with his great vision to see what foods there are for Spexman. Liklik, you see, was a slave, he was held in bondage by Spexman, the dragon. Liklik had to do the dragon's bidding or Spexman would wipe his kind off the face of the earth for good – an agreement that Liklik dare not break.

Coyote had to find a way to enlist the help of Liklik.

Coyote figured out Spexman never wanted to eat a coyote – that was like a hairball he didn't need. Nobody wanted Coyote as food. Nothing eats coyote, you know. And so, Coyote shows himself to Liklik and cries out, *Look Look Look!*

Then soon Coyote's putting on different guises to draw Liklik in. The Sparrow Hawk warily hovers over him. Coyote yells out. *Come here! Come here! I got something special to show you… you have to come closer!* So Liklik, being curious, flies down and lands a safe distance away. Coyote tells him, he says, *You want to see something you've never seen before?*

Suddenly up jumps one of the boys.... then a second later, the other! Liklik says, *I've seen people before but I've never seen any that are alike.*

Coyote then tells Liklik,
You've got to help us. We will set you free if you help us rid the world of Spexman.

Ohh.... ahhh.... well.... Liklik hesitates, *I don't know, I don't know. That's a power, that's a power that no one else has.*

We do! Red Star and Blue Star tell him. And so, he is recruited.

RED STAR AND BLUE STAR ATTACK SPEXMAN

The boys position themselves a ways upriver and come floating down on two logs. Before getting to Spexman they split up. Silently, one goes to one side of rocky shoreline and the other makes his way to the opposite shore. They wait. Liklik sees them and lets out his scream alerting his master – *yiiiiii yhaaa.*

In an instant, Spexman rises above the water and looks around. Spexman, you see, is Elemental. He's Water. He's Vapor. He's Fog. He is Lightning. He is everything, an all-powerful Shapeshifter. That's the power that Red Star and Blue Star alongside Liklik have to reckon with. Upon hearing the signal Spexman turns around and spots this nice soft, tasty young boy standing by the shore, just waiting to be eaten... standing there with only a stick in his hand.

Spexman dives under the water and suddenly rises to claim and eat that little boy. Immediately, Blue Star dives into a hole. Simultaneously, Red Star rises from the other side of the river,

Red Star hollers at Spexman, taunting him, *Over here, over here!* The Dragon Monster turns. *Whooa! They're fast.* Spexman dives underwater and quickly goes toward Red Star. *What??? He's gone!!!*

Back along the other side of the river Blue Star rises again and yells at Spexman, *Over here, over here!* It happens again and again, back and forth… back and forth…. Spexman didn't know he was dealing with two. He thought he was dealing with one who had some special power but he couldn't figure it out. Man was puny; he never knew man to have Power. Certainly, boys don't have Power! They don't have medicine. They have no šúmáx no məryám.

19

SPEXMAN'S BLOOD TRAIL
EARTHQUAKE POINT

The battle begins. One Twin throws his spear; its sharp point hits the water dragon, slicing one of its enormous eyes. Spexman lets out a bellowing roar... He roars and screams, rises from the water, takes flight, and charges up the river. Spexman dives into rock, flying deep within. Through the rock and out again at Ribbon Cliff, screaming, climbing, clawing up the cliff's massive walls, leaving a blood trail along the cliff.

William Layman

SPEXMAN'S TAIL
GOOSETAIL ROCK

The shrieking Spexman takes to the air again, screaming, flying
upriver, growing in size, fury and rage. He has to lighten his load –
he's way too big by then. He breaks off his tail up beyond the base
of Knapps Hill. *Let that go, I don't need that!* It is known today as
Goosetail Rock.

Going back downriver Spexman shrieks and screams. He is beyond
anger – a rage like no other. Spexman rises out of the water, turns into
Vapor… into a cloud. He strikes down as Lightning – all around the
heavens light up, like arrows raining from the sky. Nowhere, nowhere
are the Twins to be found. Then Blue Star and Red Star suddenly rise
again. Now Spexman figures it out. He too rises, he rises from the
water… pulling in water… pulling in energy and more energy, getting
ready to fry them, cook them. Just then he hears a sound in front of
him, a loud buzzing and whirring....

It's Hummingbird (čəx̌ppəmpəm̓) , the smallest
but greatest warrior of them all! Pum Pum had
been spending days preparing for war, sharpening
his beak for Spexman. When Spexman lost the one
eye, Pum Pum would not leave that eye alone. You
know, how when you've got something in front of your eye, you can't
focus, it drives you mad? There Hummingbird remained, making
Spexman all the madder.

SPEXMAN'S HEAD IN MIDDLE OF RIVER

TURN PAGE UPSIDE DOWN – IN THE HOLE YOU WILL SEE LIKLIK

Spexman looks up. He leans back.... he hears a sound. Ah, it's his friend Liklik. Down from the heavens dives Liklik – Sparrowhawk! Liklik – Arrow from the Light! Liklik – Dragon Slayer! Liklik rips Spexman's other eyeball out. Blue Star and Red Star quickly thrust spears repeatedly into his soft belly. After many spears the monster is subdued. Defeated, Spexman sinks into the water where he turns to stone. When the river recedes, the head (q̇ʷúmqən) emerged from the dark water and is there now in the middle of the Columbia. Near the top of that rock is a hole. Inside that hole Liklik builds his nest.

SPEXMAN'S RIBS AND SPINE
STEMILT PINNACLES

To the west, are the Stemilt Pinnacles. That's Spexman's spine (šnakʷəptəəllqs) and rib cage (čək̓áɬp).

SPEXMAN'S CLAW
EAST BANK COLUMBIA RIVER

A short distance upriver Spexman's claw (yapcʼəlx̌ʷš) rises
from the river's east bank.

Just above Wenatchee everyone sees Saddle Rock as Black Bear and Grizzly Bear, turned into stone by Coyote.

When Native Wenatchi/P'squosa people look at the spires, they also see Spexman's horns.

The People were freed.
When you look up above Wenatchee
you see Twin Peaks.

Red Star and Blue Star are there,
watching over the valley.